M000015322

This book belongs to:

____

Made in the USA
Coppell, TX
27 February 2022

74192759R00066